Hospice of Faith

by Christina LaCross,

A Christian Hospice Nurse

Cover artwork by © 2009 Helen Bolton

Used by permission.

Scripture references are from the King James Version.

Bolton Publishing LLC

ISBN: 978-0-9855312-6-3

Table of Contents

INTRODUCTION

This book proves that even when we believe ourselves to be insufficient, God can make things happen. I don't read books, and I know that I should be the last person on earth to write a book. The idea of writing a book came about when I expressed to a patient of mine that I wrote my experiences down so I would never forget them. We were having a conversation about why I was a hospice nurse. She was a sweet, encouraging patient who I will never forget. As a matter of fact, I felt my time with her was so short. She told me she would love to read my stories, and so I started thinking that if my experiences can help others stay strong in their faith, then it's worth trying to make my stories into a book rather than just my journal.

If you are like me and just want to dive into the juicy stuff, skip the introduction and go to the first chapter. The stories are what this book is about, not me. But for those who wonder who I am and why I wrote this book, please continue on.

I love my testimony about getting my hospice job. I actually went to nursing school to be a hospice nurse; however, when I was a young nurse, I had a more experienced nurse inform me that only registered nurses could be hospice nurses. Well, that made me put my dream on the back burner for a while. I felt that, with raising my children, I could not go back to school. I settled into a clinic job after I gained my experience from the hospital. I knew I was not satisfied with that career. Clinic nurses have my blessing! They are overworked and underpaid. So I ended up working a lot of overtime doing something I hated. My family seemed to be drawing more distant, not talking as much as we should, no meals were ever together, and it was just frustrating, to say the least. I was always missing school events and felt like I was rushing today to get ready for tomorrow, day after day.

After seeking God's plan for my life, I felt He was leading me to go to a part-time position at the clinic instead of full time. It did not make sense at the time; we flat could not afford it. Why would I cut my pay when we could barely make ends meet as it was? But God knew what He was doing. I felt as if I was stepping off a cliff and, with my faith, Jesus would be there to catch me. As it turned out, two weeks to the day after I started working part time, a former co-worker of mine came into the clinic. I had actually worked under her at the hospital and loved her. She was always sweet and full of sunshine. She lit up a room when she walked in. She was now working for a hospice company.

You can probably see where this is going. She asked me how I was doing, so I started explaining, and when I told her I was working part time, the papers she had in her hand flew across the counter, knocking everything over. She stumbled over her words and asked me, in a whisper, if I wanted another part-time job. When I explained that I was only a licensed vocational nurse, she said "So what?"

That is where my journey of a lifetime began. I sent in an application and was hired immediately. Since it was hospice, there were so many different things I had to do before I could actually care for patients. There were physicals and a lot of orientation that I had to start immediately. As it turned out, I was able to complete everything by working a half day at the clinic, then doing orientation for hospice the rest of the day. If I had not been part time, there would have been no way I could have completed everything in the appropriate time frame. Funny how God is in control all the time, but we question

Him when it doesn't make sense to us. This is why I'm choosing to call this book *Hospice of Faith*. When I stepped off that cliff with faith, Jesus caught me and brought me where He wanted me to be.

It was an eye-opening experience when I was training for my hospice position. During this time I had the opportunity to meet a really great person. He was the administrator of our company and I was so nervous to have to meet him. I will never forget sitting across from him at his huge desk in his office. I already had the job, but I felt like I had to impress him. I was sweating and tongue-tied. He asked me why I wanted to be a hospice nurse. I gave my testimony and he seemed to like it. He then said the most shocking thing I've ever heard a boss say. He said "Christy, the most important thing to me is to make sure all of our patients have a chance to accept Jesus Christ as their Lord and Savior before they die." Isn't that the most amazing statement from a boss? I knew then and there that God had plans and I needed to let Him lead and guide me into this new journey. I shook my head all the way home. Do I really have a job this good? I thanked God over and over. He gave me something I didn't deserve, but really wanted. I am so passionate about my faith and my experiences that I wanted to share some of my wonderful memories. Although my patient that is responsible for this book is not here to read this, maybe someone like her can enjoy it. I could not have done it alone. I thank God for these memories.

As much as I value each patient for their uniqueness and experience, I must only refer to them as "patients" or make up a new name for them. I hate the thought of giving them another name, so I will just call them my "patients." These stories are all true, even though they may seem unbelievable. I have eliminated identifying information in order to protect my patients' privacy.

God cares so much about His children that He even cares about their death. The journey toward death can be a very cruel and hard situation, especially on the physical body. Watching your loved one pass from this world with some kind of disease, such as cancer, can be more than a person can handle. I want to share just how amazing God really is. I do not want to take any credit for anything that I did in these stories. God helped me the whole way. I constantly ask Him to please lead and guide me to do His will. Some are pure mysteries. I have discovered that God does not want anyone to know when someone will pass. Just when we think we have it figured out, God changes things. He wants us all to know that He is in control. I feel so blessed by these occurrences and hope they bless you as well. God is so good!

Christina LaCross

The Bright Light

The very first time I witnessed the actual passing of one of my patients, I was amazed. I usually get called after the death occurs. This one particular patient was definitely declined and it was apparent he was going to the Lord this very day. I happened to be at the facility where he was when the family asked me to stay. I was more than happy to do so, and offered comfort to the family.

After being at the facility for about six hours, I was called into the patient's room. He was on his way to Heaven. As we were all gathered around his bed, he lifted his right arm briefly, opened and closed his eyes quickly, looking straight above, and then stopped breathing. It was as if he saw something and grabbed for it. He hadn't opened his eyes in days. What caused him to suddenly open his eyes for just a moment? I felt chills as he left his body. I was holding his hand and remember feeling so honored to be in that moment.

Don't Talk to Me About Jesus

One story that really stands out is about a patient that had a recurrent disease. She was a retired nurse and didn't hold anything back. She told you exactly what she thought! The dreaded day came when she slowly declined. There was an evening that I was called to go and check on her. She had some anxiety, so she was given some medication. If you know much about hospice, you know it's pretty common for people to have anxiety and agitation toward the end of life.

During this visit it was just me and the patient. As I sat in a chair beside her bed waiting for her medications to take effect, she was voicing some very disturbing thoughts. Although she was stern, she was never mean, so I knew something was wrong. You could tell she was troubled. I was told that sometimes this is a spiritual battle. I asked her if she knew Jesus. She said, "I hate Jesus. Don't talk to me about Jesus." And then she said it again.

This really bothered me. I stood up beside her bed. I pleaded the blood of Jesus over me and I began to speak to her. I just knew that if she passed away that night, she would have some regrets, and so would I. I was terribly nervous. I had never encountered this before. I was having that little quiet talk with Jesus, asking if He was going to help me out. I knew I must do something, so I took her by the hand and asked her if I could pray for her. She resentfully agreed. I had never prayed out loud before! So here I am again, taking a step off that cliff and hoping Jesus is there! I started rambling off a prayer that I didn't think was in me. I was just asking God for His forgiveness and understanding. I asked Him to penetrate her heart with His love. I asked her to accept Him as her

Lord and Savior. I rebuked any spirit that wasn't of God. The whole time I'm praying, she is lying there with her eyes closed not saying a word.

I didn't know what was going to happen next. It was quiet for what seemed like an eternity. She then opened her eyes and, in a quiet little voice, said, "Thank you, Christy." My heart melted. At that point I said, "Do you know where you're going after you die?" She said, with a smile, "Yes, I'm going to Heaven," and we both cried. And I said, with all authority, "Yes ma'am, you are!" She was very peaceful after that Wednesday, but never spoke again. She went to be with her Lord that very Saturday. She never needed anymore medications to keep her comfortable. She had a very peaceful exit with her daughter holding her hand.

A week later I returned to the home for some donated supplies. While I was there, the daughter expressed her sadness of not knowing if her mother accepted Jesus before she died. I was quick to share the story of what happened that Wednesday before her mother passed. The daughter immediately cried and said she was so worried about her mom's salvation. Unfortunately, not all families like to hear about their loved ones spiritual needs. Not everyone believes in Jesus and how He has saved us. It was a great relief for the daughter to hear this story. I can't imagine how upsetting it would be to think your loved one didn't make Heaven.

The Presence of a Calming Peace

I was called to check on a patient. She was having difficulty breathing. She had been battling a terminal diagnosis for years, but we had only had her as a patient for a week when I was called over. Over the last few days she had steadily declined. Our chaplain went to pray for the patient, and soon thereafter her breathing changed. Breathing can become irregular as a person gets closer to death. When I went to check on her, I noticed that she had a rattle when she breathed. She was repositioned, suctioned, and medicated, all in attempts to have her reach a level of comfort. All the while, I'm asking God to help me help her.

She did seem to have a little anxiety, but not too bad. I asked the two daughters to please step out of the room so the husband could have some time alone with his wife. Sometimes my patients need to hear that it is okay for them to pass from the one they are closest to. Just a short time after her husband stepped out of her room; we heard the patient cough so we went back in the bedroom where she was sleeping. She needed more medication, and then she seemed peaceful again.

Her breathing had changed again at this point. After feeling an overwhelming nudge from the Holy Spirit, I told her husband that it wouldn't be much longer. Sometimes I look back and am in awe of how God works. I just always want to be in the right place at the right time so God can use me.

Her oldest daughter began to pray while holding her mom's hand. A short time later, maybe three minutes, the younger daughter held the other hand. The husband, both daughters and I were all in the bedroom at this time. With the lights dim, the patient's eyes, that hadn't opened in three days, popped open. She stared straight north for just a brief second, then closed her eyes and stopped breathing. I believe she saw the brightest light she's ever seen.

I felt chills all over my body as she exited. You could feel the presence of a calming peace. It was an awesome work of God. I feel so honored to be a part of that experience. I do feel that God chooses certain people for certain times. I thank Him for using me.

It's Not Over until God Says It's Over

I arrived for a routine visit on this particular patient. I knew she was not saved, so that made this moment huge in my book. I knocked on the door and after several minutes the patient's husband let me in. He was very groggy and sat in his chair to go back to sleep.

When I saw my patient, who was lying in a bed that was in the living room, I knew it wasn't good. We'd only had this patient briefly, but she had taken a huge turn for the worse since I had last seen her. I started medications to calm her. She was having difficulty breathing. It was clear that this lady had only a few precious moments before she died. In addition to having difficulty breathing, she was extremely agitated.

I felt God's pull to grab her hand, and then I spoke to her. I told her she was about die and that she needed to make things right with God. She was unable to speak, but was constantly moving in agitation. I said a sinner's prayer with her. Her husband was sitting in the room and it was a little nerve-racking not knowing what he thought about me trying to save his wife's soul. Nevertheless, it had to be done. God put me there for a reason. After I prayed with her, she immediately calmed down. She had a peace come over her, and I was able to notify family members that she didn't have much longer.

It wasn't long before all of her family came in crying and upset. They were all in denial and loved her too much to let her go. They were talking loud and making plans for fun things to do later with her. The tension soon caused my patient to become a fighter. Not good for a patient who can't breathe. Luckily my co-worker had arrived by this time giving us an opportunity to have the family step out of the room while we cleaned up our patient. This was it! This was the opportunity to pray for God to intervene and stop her suffering. She was having such difficulty breathing that it was making my stomach turn, so my co-worker and I started praying! We closed our prayers and quickly cleaned the patient. The patient finally reached a calming peace again.

The family was asked to come back in, but to please be very calm and quiet. The patient did have a couple of moments of awareness after that. Within ten minutes, that sweet lady went to be with Jesus. Her family was surrounding the bed and holding her hand. Although that wasn't the perfect hospice death, it was exactly what needed to happen for this patient to find salvation.

I believe some people are very strong willed and deeply hurt. Life causes a lot of pain that prevents people from having a good relationship with God. God's grace is bigger than we can ever imagine. I wish everyone could just believe that. Was it God's will for her to suffer, or was God sending me to help her in her hour of need? I was not scheduled to see this patient until hours later, but circumstances changed my schedule that day.

I Want to Go Home

This is a sweet story. Unfortunately, we had this patient for only a short time. The family was one of the coolest families you could imagine. They were very laid back and tried to offer beers to everyone that came over.

I got called to go check on this patient one morning. She was clearly going to see Jesus soon. She was doing a lot of moaning, but couldn't tell us if she was in pain. She did have a very small amount of medication in case she was hurting, but the moaning never went away. You may have heard of the calm before the storm. Well, this is a good example of it.

After being at the patient's house for more than an hour observing her and trying to figure out why she was moaning, it became apparent what was happening. She had all her children in the room. She started struggling to speak. She would start to say something, and it wouldn't come out. She would then start moaning again. Finally after 30 minutes she struggled to say, "I want to go home." The family just made light of it and said, "You are home. We are all here and you're going to be okay."

She immediately lifted her left arm and pointed with one finger toward the ceiling as she struggled to say, "No." The tears began to fall in that room, myself included. She then moaned for another 15 minutes before her son, who was getting frustrated, said "Mom, I love you". As clear as a bell --remember she had been struggling to say something for 15 minutes -- she said, "I love you, too." She struggled another 15 minutes and finally said, "I love everyone." A big sigh of relief came across her face. After she was able to say that, she no longer moaned or struggled to say anything else and went peacefully on to be with the Lord that night.

The love of this mother was strong, even to the end. Even though they were grown, her kids needed to hear and she needed to say, "I love you," one last time.

Tell Jesus Hello

This was a cute patient we had for a while. When her number came up, she was ready. She was full of such spunk, even to the end. I had a very difficult time with this death. This was the first time I saw a patient take her last breath while alert and oriented. I don't care to ever see that again. Unfortunately, she was unable to take the medications that are used to make a patient sleep through this transition.

During the last minutes of her life, I was asked by a co-worker who could not be there to please tell our patient to tell Jesus hello for her. Well, during this all serious, gloomy moment, my patient speaks up in a loud, straight-forward voice and says, "Anyone else want me to tell Him anything?" Wow, it took that room by surprise. We all started laughing. She did, too, and it wasn't much longer before she passed.

How does someone on their deathbed keep their sense of humor? It is amazing to me, truly amazing.

Waiting Buzzards

Here is another funny incident. I had this little lady and, again, thought she was an awesome, inspirational lady. Her day came and she was lying in bed with all her family gathered around. I must say there was a lot of family and they were always gathered around her bed. Sometimes I even thought it was a little overbearing.

The day she passed she hadn't spoken in a couple of days, but she got a boost of energy in her last moments and told everyone, "Quit standing around like a bunch of buzzards waiting on something to die." It blew my mind. I wasn't sure if it was okay to laugh or not. I sure laughed about it later, though.

This same lady would speak of seeing her husband, who had passed several years back. I hear it all the time. People who are soon to pass over into another place will see their loved ones, little children, or even really pretty sceneries. God truly cares about us. He allows us peace at even the most difficult times of our lives.

Can't Tie God's Hands

Here's another wonderful story of a gentleman I took care of. The day we admitted this patient, we were all informed that the patient and family are very firm on not mentioning anything about God or Jesus. It puzzles me why some people are so against such a loving God. Nevertheless, we can't mention it, but no one said we couldn't pray for this man. Sometimes I think my job is to just pray for my patient. I may be the only one who is, so I did pray, and prayed hard. My heart really does ache for someone who does not know Jesus the way I do. He is my best friend and he helps me during the "crisis" times. I never panic; I just do what I'm led to do.

So, here it is. I was called because this patient didn't look good and was having difficulty breathing. I get there and his sitter of many years is by his side. He has a daughter who is present, but his son is on the way. My patient was going down fast. I asked if there was anyone who wanted to be alone with this patient to say any final goodbyes, and the sitter spoke up and said she would, please, like a minute. I encouraged the daughter to let the sitter have some time. The daughter agreed and went to another room with me.

When the sitter came out, the daughter went back in to hold his hand. As soon as their hands touched, he took his last breath. Remember, my hands were tied. The family made their demands known. All I could do is quietly pray for him, asking God for guidance, but feeling like there was nothing I could do.

What ended up happening was truly awesome. The son, who is not a nice man, to say it mildly, came through the back door three minutes after his father passed. This is very rare. For some reason, a person can will

14

themselves to stay alive for a loved one to make it to them to say goodbye. The family was openly grieving. The son was very upset that he didn't make it in time to say goodbye. The daughter was consoling her brother stating, "Dad tried to wait on you."

A short time later, I was in the living room with the sitter, who is also a Christian. She started telling me about saying a sinner's prayer with my patient. She knew she would not get another chance, so she went for it. She said she was so nervous that the family would come in and be upset with her. Instead, what happened was that the patient was prayed with and accepted Jesus during that brief moment that the sitter was with him.

I believe that God knew my patient might change his mind once the rough and rowdy son got there, so God took him while He had him. I believe prayers rang in heaven and God found a way. Could this be a coincidence? It's possible. It depends on what you believe. I will always believe that families can tie my hands, but they can't tie God's hands.

Really Bad End

I am a true believer that God speaks to people; maybe not in an audible voice, but through His sweet Spirit. If you had been there for this experience, you might believe it, too.

This precious lady was a very rooted, spirit-filled Christian who taught me so much. Even though it was my job to teach her, she actually taught me about life. There's a saying that states, "If you want to know how to live, ask someone who is dying." That is so true. This patient actually dealt with her illness using the power of denial. She insisted on focusing on "other" things. When we would go visit her, she didn't want to discuss nausea, vomiting, bowel issues, pain, etc. She liked to pretend we were just there for a friendly visit. She constantly redirected questions and asked us about our lives. It was almost therapeutic for her to hear about someone else's life. She had such a strong will; nevertheless, her illness started staking its claim when she had been on our services for a long period of time. She spoke of hearing a sweet voice that told her that "the end will be really bad, but it won't last very long." Sure enough, those words came to pass.

Our team did all we could, but she was in so much pain. She had been on narcotics for so long that her body was requiring more than we could give her. There is a cap on medications and how much can be given. We had reached that cap. My heart broke for her. I still don't understand why God knew this would be, but did nothing to change it. It was so true; the end was really bad, but it was true that she was only in bed for three days. Three days is actually quick for a young body to die.

I feel that sometimes when a family is very close to their loved one, it's so hard to let go. Somehow we, as humans, can justify a loved one dying if they were suffering. Maybe that's why some suffer? I may never know why this ended the way it did, but I do know Who is in control.

My Own Experience

I guess if I'm going to write about my hospice experiences, I really should include the story of when I had to place my own mother on hospice. She had a horrible disease of twenty years and was miserable most of the time. I watched her decline through the years. I could write a book on just that experience alone.

I got a call one Monday morning from my co-worker stating that, as much as she hated to tell me, my mother had taken a turn and was doing very poorly. I had mixed emotions, for sure. I immediately went to my mother's side. Since I had been a hospice nurse for so long, I was thinking like a nurse instead of a daughter. I was focused on her medical issues rather than realizing my siblings needed to be called. So I paused, asked Jesus to help me through this, and proceeded to inform my siblings.

I ended up taking time off of work so I could be with my momma. She was no longer responding. It was very clear that she would be leaving this world soon. It was as if I was in a dream. Is this really happening? Is it my turn in life to deal with personally what I have been dealing with professionally for so long?

I have a sister that lives in another state who had come down and spent a week with our mother prior to this day. I heard several stories about how Mother was talking and communicating better than ever while she was here. Mother had received the "burst of energy." My sister, who I quickly called to inform of mother's condition, was totally surprised and didn't understand. I explained that mother had not been that energetic in months. Again, I felt pulled to explain the burst of energy rather than just be the daughter.

I then called my other sister and my only brother. We made a family decision to spend this precious time with Mother by ourselves. We did not call anyone else. Mother had been sick and unable to communicate for years, therefore was not very close to many people.

The experience I want to share is how I became a patient's family instead of a hospice nurse. I sat holding Momma's hand, which I cherish so much. I even snapped a picture of me holding her hand. It was as if I wanted to save every moment I could. My siblings and I would take turns being with her. I became extremely worn out very fast. I thought to myself, "Is this what my patient's family members experience?" It's very draining, both physically and mentally. I knew it was difficult, but I didn't realize the magnitude of it.

With mother's oxygen concentrator running and all the nursing home noise, I wasn't getting any sleep. I was torn between knowing I needed rest and not wanting Mother to die without me there. I now have a great appreciation for families that muster up the will to be by their loved one's side. I couldn't even spend one night!

Soon after midnight, I had all I could take. I told my mother I would be back in the morning. I returned at 6:00 the following morning. Nothing had changed. She was still going through the process. A little piece of me was wishing it was a dream. As much as I hated to see her sick all these years, I hated to think of life without her. After I was there with my mother for an hour that morning, I felt the need to pray. So I did what any young Christian would do, I called another relative to come pray. That's about right, huh? He said the prettiest, most peaceful prayer about God taking mother home soon. Soon after he left, I felt like I was being led to get my Bible and read the Lord's Prayer to her. I had so many tears in my eyes, it was difficult to see. I was glad I actually had some of it memorized.

In less than thirty minutes I was sitting down, holding her hand and praying a soft prayer for the Lord to please put an end to her suffering. She was breathing loud through all of the congestion. I suddenly felt the presence of that sweet, peaceful spirit enter the room. I spoke to Momma and said, "They are here to get you. I love you. It's time for you to go now."

Suddenly her breathing changed, and within a minute she took her last breath. It was totally amazing to me. My faith acknowledges that supernatural events occur. I remember not ever hesitating to tell her, "They are here to get you." If I had thought about it any longer, I might have hesitated to speak that, but I knew what I felt because I had felt it before. I no longer had any desire to hold the shell of my mom's spirit.

I have a special peace in knowing where she went. I would not trade that experience for anything in the world. I believe my experience of being a hospice nurse was a benefit to me. I can't imagine being a hospice nurse without being able to walk hand in hand daily with Jesus Christ.

Is Accepting Hospice Denying God's Power?

This was a wild ride for sure! I was called to go on a consult one evening. This gentleman was barely clinging on to life. He had two oxygen concentrators hooked up to him and was still struggling. He had been battling this disease for years. He was very aware of his surroundings and illness. He was able to carry on a respectable conversation, slowly. If he spoke too fast, he became short of breath.

The family wanted hospice to come in, but the patient had a lot of reservations. After an hour of talking with this patient and getting to know him, he bluntly asked me a question. I really felt inadequate to counsel anyone, but I truly believe God gives me words when I have none. His question to me was, "If I say it is okay for hospice to come in, am I telling God that I don't believe He will heal me?" Wow! At this point in time I really wanted someone else to be answering this question, but God stepped in and I had the words that man needed to hear. I told him, "God knows the heart. He knows you love Him and trust Him. Sometimes we think that our healing has to be done here on earth. God's will and man's will may not be the same. I believe God chooses to heal some of us by letting us go to Heaven. Your faith is not waivered by facing reality that your healing is coming when you get to Heaven. God's grace and mercy is more powerful than that."

I believe that man found true peace after our conversation. His wife later shared that he didn't talk much that night, only to tell his wife he truly loved her and he was okay with hospice coming in to help him out.

The wife said that at 3:00 in the morning, after going to bed at 10.00 the night before, his breathing changed and he became unresponsive. Later that morning the wife called wanting our services. By the time we were able to come; he was having a very hard time and struggling for air. We went to work and made him comfortable. It was very evident that he would be leaving this world soon.

Once again, with the Holy Spirit guiding me, I informed the wife that he would not be with us much longer. His wife was holding his hand while he was relaxed in his favorite recliner. The best part of this story was when I felt that sweet spirit enter the room. I looked at his wife, who was looking at me. He then took his last breath. His wife later confirmed that when we looked at each other, we were both feeling that wonderful, sweet spirit that embraced the room. It is like no other feeling on earth.

I cannot wait to have eternity that will be full of nothing but that sweet peaceful and warming spirit. I can't wait to see the place God has prepared for me. I'm sure I'm going to love it!

Fireworks and Pastures

This was pretty incredible to me. I was having a discussion one day with my nephew, who is studying engineering at college. He informed me of a synthetic chemical that people extract from plants called DMT. After doing a little -- and I do mean a little -- bit of research on the chemical, I was floored. There is a chemical in the human brain that is released when a person is born, when they die, or have a very traumatic event.

People have tampered with this synthetic version of DMT, only to find some wild results. When DMT is shot into the human vein, the person is rendered helpless and proceeds to have full 3D visions that are in bright colors. The colors are like none here on earth. It's described like a trip from LSD. The words they use to describe the experience are weak compared to the actual experience. After injecting this chemical more than two times, a person will have a very negative, evil experience that is traumatic for the person, so bad that they will not attempt to use the chemical again. It sounds to me like God does not want this experience to happen casually.

Now, there are people that smoke DMT, but the effects are not as vivid as the trip where it is injected into the bloodstream where God intended the chemical to be. It can even be eaten, but the effects are very weak that way.

So I wonder why God made such a chemical to be released from the brain at these times of transition. My belief is that it could be such a shock to go from one world into another that he uses DMT to give snapshots of what's to come after death.

One such example would be when a patient on his death bed smiled at me and struggled to tell me he'd had a dream. Usually during a patient's last moments, they are extremely weak, so I pay special attention to what my patients feel the need to say at this point. So he stated that the dream was of the biggest, most beautiful fireworks he had ever seen. He said, "I think the grand finale will be tonight." Was that God's way of preparing him for what was coming?

I'm not sure why we have this special gift of DMT, but I see it all the time. I had a sweet, Christian lady tell me one time when she was close to passing that the grass is so green and beautiful. She said, "I wish you could see just how amazing it is." This is someone that has a good reason to be doom and gloom, but instead she is floating on clouds as happy as she can be. Some believe it's because a lot of hospice patients have to take pain medicines to control symptoms, and that's why they hallucinate. Well, I will tell you from experience that I have seen many patients not taking medications, such as this past lady, that still had the same experience of seeing the beautiful scenes.

It is tearful and humbling to hear them speak of another place. I look forward to seeing it myself someday. If it wasn't for my family, I would be ready today. I am convinced that whatever is on the other side is far better than what is on this side.

It's Okay to Just Be Quiet

I had the honor of caring for a lady that taught me that friends are great, but not always appreciated. She would tell me, "My friends just don't understand. They think they are doing me a favor by constantly taking turns coming to visit or play cards, but I just mostly want to be left alone." She asked me if that was a bad thing or not. I felt that, under the circumstances, that was very appropriate. She did not want to seem rude so she never spoke up, but the situation never changed. She would tell me that she liked when I came because her friends and family left and I didn't talk a lot.

When she told me that, I remembered years prior when I was in nursing school and I had taken care of her husband. He was a witty man who struggled to speak. This particular day it was my turn to sit with him on the porch so he could smoke. I wheeled him outside to enjoy the sunshine and cigarette. I wasn't much on small talk, but managed to make a few statements about the weather. I remember thinking to myself, "I have to think of something else to talk about," but nothing really came to mind. I sat quietly for a moment, and then I spoke up and said, "You know, sometimes I think it's best to just sit and enjoy the quiet." He smiled the biggest smile and struggled to say, "Yes, ma'am, it is." We enjoyed our time outside without any other words being said. He seemed very pleased to have enjoyed quiet time outside listening to the birds. He changed my view on taking care of patients. Talking just to be talking is not always what a patient needs. Sometimes it's just the presence of someone, not the noise they make.

When I shared that with his wife, she thought it was pretty special. Just because someone is going through a hard time doesn't necessarily mean they want to stay busy with friends and conversation. It can be a challenge to meet a patient's needs, especially if you believe they all want to sit and talk.

Can You Will Yourself to Die?

This next patient allowed me to realize just how important a person's will to live can be. A few times I have witnessed patients being sent home on hospice with a diagnosis that will not end their life anytime soon, but for some reason they just give up.

We had a patient with just that situation. No matter how much we encouraged and educated, she believed she was dying soon. Can a person will themselves to die? In giving up, a person may stop eating, drinking, and withdraw from loved ones. Within a week, that poor lady passed. I just don't get it. It's hard to understand why someone gives up. It is then that I have to realize that this individual may have been fighting for years to beat this disease, and now that she knows she will not win, is her fight gone? Is that why people lose their will to live?

Messing with God's Plan

A patient of mine was unable to speak due to a debilitating condition. Her daughter was present when I arrived for my first visit. I spoke with the daughter. She was grieving and asking why God would do this to a faithful woman of God. She proceeded to tell me how her mother was in charge of so much at the church she had attended her whole life. She had even brought up all her kids in church. The daughter said, "My mother looks scared because she can't communicate." She said, "I can't handle my mother being like this. I'm getting mad at God."

Again, I had to ask God to lead and guide me on what to tell this poor daughter. These are very delicate situations and could cause someone to waiver in their faith. I ended up asking the daughter if she had prayed for God's will to be done? I asked if I could pray with her, and she agreed. I asked God to please heal her or take her home. I mentioned that the daughter needed comfort and understanding. It turned out to be an awesome prayer, and the daughter thanked me.

The very next day that patient went home to be with the Lord. I know this may be coincidental but not to me. I believe God heard our prayer and did all He could to make it right. Maybe her daughter just needed a way to make letting go a little easier. Maybe it was really the patient's time to go when she had been rushed to the hospital where they saved her life instead of allowing her to peacefully die the way God intended.

I believe sometimes modern medicine gets in the way of God's plans. "When He puts His hands on them,

we need to take our hands off of them." I like that saying.
I didn't make it up, but I like it.

Difficulty Controlling Pain

I was a new hospice nurse when I had this
experience. I was called to a patient's house because she
was very agitated and had a lot of pain. I was new, so
there was a little nervousness going on, but I was
confident that God would see me through.

After being there two hours and giving a very high
dose of pain medication, the patient still was not
comfortable. I proceeded to call my doctor, who informed
me that I needed to give even more medicine. I was
freaked out! He did explain to me then that patients that
have taken high doses of pain medications in their lifetime
sometimes have difficulty controlling terminal pain with
normal doses of pain medications. I am thinking at this
time, "Great, God, thanks for letting me be called to this
one." It was more than awful having family members
standing around wondering why I can't stop this lady's
pain even though I have been giving her medications.
How do you explain why it's not working to a family
member without them feeling like I'm calling her a drug
addict, or worse.

So I get off the phone with the doctor and do
exactly what I was told to do; I gave even more
medication. I felt sick to my stomach doing it. So now
I'm pleading with God to please help this poor lady. I do
feel that God doesn't want His children to suffer like this,
and I know enough about medications to know that my

patient needs relief even if it makes her incoherent or sleepy. That's where morals and values come into play. Do I continue to give this lady high doses of pain medications to control her pain and let her rest or let her suffer? It doesn't take long to realize what is right after hearing someone on their death bed moan out in pain and unable to lay still because they are in so much pain.

So, yes, I gave the medications like I needed to. That lady passed two days later with a peaceful death. It is times like this that I do a lot of talking to God to make sure I am doing His will. I only want to do what's right and never have any regrets.

Granddaughter's Card

I had a patient that was very close to passing. This was a very strong, bonded family. They prayed together and loved each other very much. Every time I went to this house, I felt so welcomed and wanted. It was exactly what I think a family should be. The grandchildren were the prized possessions in this house. They never failed to get up into the laps of their grandparents when they came over for a visit.

One evening while I was there, I witnessed something that crumbled me for days. The grandkids had been gone from the house all day and arrived while I was there. A very cute, charming four-year-old little girl came running into her grandpa's room where I was present. Grandpa only had hours or days left in this world. The little girl was so excited about what she had worked on for Grandpa all day. She came running around the corner, stared at his face and said. "Grandpa, Grandpa, I made you something." He gave it all he had to lean forward and grab the object. He then opens this crafty little construction paper card and read out loud, "I will miss you."

Do you need a minute to take that in? I did! It was very hard to keep the tears back. This little girl said so much in those four words. It totally broke my heart to know that a little girl loved her grandpa so much and knew that she would be losing him soon.

Playing with His Knee

There was a couple who was just as cute as they could be. The husband had taken care of his wife most of their lives. He had cooked, cleaned and showered her with attention. Now the wife had to care for the husband who had become bedridden. It is often difficult for the person who was the care giver to become the receiver.

His wife was so sweet, but did not understand some things. His wife explained to me one day that he was seeing people that died a long time ago. She stated that she just thought he was crazy. I reassured her that he probably was seeing such things and that it was okay. She said it scared her, so I told her there was nothing to be afraid of. She said, "Well, if you say it is okay, then I won't be scared." I find it hard to believe that there are people that haven't heard of encounters with the other side. There are, and I am now trying to convince this wife that it's normal. I know, all in a day's work, right?

So here is what occurred next. I was called to this patient's house because he was going crazy and throwing pillows off his bed. I walked in to see him very angry and throwing another pillow off of his bed. He was unable to get out of bed, but he was trying to get someone's attention. I asked him why he was angry. I had to ask in several different ways since he was not answering me. He finally spoke up, looked at me very sternly and said, "I'm dying." I said, "Yes sir, you are. Is that why you are so angry?" He said, "But I know I'm dying, and I see my brothers (who have passed), but she thinks I'm just crazy. I'm tired of her say I'm crazy."

I reassured him that if God placed in his heart that he was going to die and he was seeing his brothers, then I believed everything he said. His face went relaxed and he said, "You do?" I said, "You are having a spiritual encounter and I think it's awesome. I know how much you miss your brothers and I bet it was nice to see them." He agreed that it was great to see them. He seemed very surprised at my reaction. He was totally alert and oriented. The only "crazy" part about him was him not understanding his experiences. I believed with my whole being that he was being prepared for his next life. I had seen it before and I had no doubts. I felt honored to be talking about his experiences with him. Just in case you were wondering, he was not taking any medications either.

I had to step out of the room to take a call as we were wrapping things up. When I came back in to talk with his wife and educate her on spiritual encounters, she told me something that melted my heart. She said her husband had called her into his room when I walked out. He told her that "The lady that just left," which was me, "she is a lot like those people I see." Now that sent chills all over me instantly. I felt a confirmation from God that

He was with me all the way. If I sit and pick it apart, it could mean several different things, but I instantly felt the meaning of it and know not to over think it. I choose to believe that God was sending a little whisper to me that I was on the right track.

Earlier that week this same patient had an encounter with a small infant playing with his knee while he was up in his wheelchair. He was swatting his knee and saying, "Go on now." That was the first time his wife told me he was crazy. I asked if they had any small children pass in the family. She answered by saying they did have an eighteen-month-old grandbaby that had passed. My mind jumped to "that's what's going on."

Usually patients will admit to one or two encounters with people who have passed. I think since this patient felt safe, he opened up and shared many of his encounters. He was tired of being called crazy. That may be the very reason why more people don't speak up when they have these encounters.

Down in a Hurry

It's incredible how God keeps the mystery of death alive. I happened to be at the nursing facility when someone yelled down the hall that one of my patients needed immediate help. Upon entering the room, I noticed she was suddenly too weak to sit up in her wheelchair, holding her head in her hand, having dry heaves, and could not stand to get into bed. She was able to stand that morning, but now sudden weakness overcame her. Our staff knew that this day would soon come since she was losing blood and was severely anemic. How it happens is always a mystery.

So we get this patient into her bed. Her blood pressure was critically low, and her legs, all the way up to her hips, were what we called "mottled." That is a dark purple or red pattern that appears on a patient's extremities when they are close to death. It's actually due to a lack of circulation. Her feet were very dark in color. It was obvious this lady was headed out in a hurry. Her family was called as we got her comfortable.

All of her family arrived the next morning, as that was the quickest they could come. I arrived, expecting to see a patient that didn't have much longer to live, but God had a different plan. This patient had only eaten a couple of bites of food at a time for the last three months, but when I walked in her room that morning, she was up in her wheelchair eating all of her breakfast. Throughout the day she ate better than she had in three months. She had energy to laugh, talk and cut up with her family.

Now, this is where faith comes in again. It's not easy to explain to a family that even though their loved one looks and feels better than they have in three months, their death is drawing closer. Sometimes this burst of energy lasts a day and sometimes it lasts a week. God is in control! Families think we are nuts sometimes for telling them that death is near when their loved one looks great.

Sure enough, this patient had a wonderful week of energy, and then she spiraled down quickly. The family was called once again, and once again they came to be by her side. She did go to Heaven this time.

I'm in awe of how God orchestrates these events. His planning allowed for the family to spend precious moments with her toward the end. God is more than awesome, and I'm so appreciative to get to witness his work.

Time to Go Back Home

Some patients touch my heart a little deeper than others sometimes. One lady in particular had an illness that kept her on our services for quite a while. She was easy to love. Well, except she had a mean, little dog that loved to bite my heels.

One thing I appreciate is all the wisdom that comes from some of my patients. She taught me a lot and gave me an appreciation for family and life. It was very interesting to me how she was only sick two months before her death. She knew she was getting weak and unable to eat. She tried the power of denial, but it didn't work for her.

After a month of knowing that she was steadily declining, she had a conversation with me. She stated that she felt the need to return to her hometown. She didn't care if she passed away on the way, but she needed to make it back home. She wanted to "talk to the man that's doing my funeral services." She wanted to make sure he would do and say what she wanted. She did not want her funeral to be sad.

Arrangements, such as providing oxygen tanks and calling a hospice in that area to help out, were made. I will always remember the day she left from our area. She didn't say goodbye. She didn't get emotional. We just gave each other a stare that said so many words. We knew that she wouldn't be back. Her health was really bad at this point, but for some reason it was too much for us to say goodbye to each other. There was a connection between us, and I remember not wanting her to go. My friend/patient relationship was coming to an end after all this time.

She made it home and was totally exhausted from the trip. She never got out of bed again. The family notified us when she passed. I drove four hours to attend her funeral. I'm not sure I will ever do that again. I guess a part of me was hoping it wasn't real and I would get to see her again. Another part of me wanted to see where this wonderful lady had grown up. The trip was worth it because the family got to tell me that my patient left a message for me. Even though we didn't say goodbye, she let me know that she really appreciated my friendship and love. I sure miss that lady, but not her dog!

"...the Battle is the LORD's..."
I Samuel 17:47

I debated with myself whether I should share this story with others. I chose to do so, since my book is based on faith and this story was a huge faith builder in my walk. I will never see life the same way again.

A co-worker of mine called me one evening to assist in admitting a patient. Not ever a problem, so I went to help. That night was the start of a journey I would never forget. My co-worker walked by and shook hands with our new patient; then I walked in a few steps behind her. I reached out to shake her hand, but she hesitated by keeping her hand to herself. It was slightly lifted, so I grabbed it with both of my hands. I thought this may be a frail lady that has trouble shaking hands, until I looked into her eyes. The moment I made eye contact, I was suddenly sick to my stomach. Her eyes became blood red

34

as she stared me down; just the whites of her eyes, which were already a little red.

I pulled back my hand, knowing I had just encountered a spirit that was unsettling to me. Never had I ever had such an encounter. The patient never spoke while I was there, although I wasn't there for very long. My coworker assured me she was fine if I was ready to leave. I felt uneasy leaving my co-worker, but she reassured me she was good. Since I was not doing so well, I was eager to get out of there.

I left that house and cried all the way home. I felt as if I had shaken the hand of Satan himself. I was asking God what that was about and why it happened. I didn't understand why it happened to me. I was scared and didn't really know how to handle this situation. That's exactly what I told my husband, who was wondering why I was shaking like a leaf when I got home.

As it turned out, I had to visit that lady the next day. I can honestly say I was not looking forward to having to go to that house again, especially since I spent the whole night tossing and turning, seeing those horrible eyes. I actually thought I would be smart and go with my aide so we would not be alone. I felt a little better about going since my aide was a spirit-filled Christian, also.

We arrived at the house all prayed up and ready to tackle whatever the day would hold for us. We went in, as we were instructed. As luck would have it, we got lost in the house first thing. It was a big house and the patient was home alone, not answering to us calling out. We finally found the bedroom where she is lying down, covered up and all alone. I made my aide go in first. That's just what I felt was right at the time. She made her way to the bed and started saying, "Good morning, time to wake up," and then described to her who we were and why we were there.

The patient finally rolled over and attempted to speak. A few garbled words came out. No threats at this time. I was feeling a little relieved. My aide stated that she would go draw some bath water while I took the patient's vital signs. Easy enough, I thought. So here we go. After taking a deep breath, I take her blood pressure and notice her skin feels warm and dry, as it should. I think so far so good, right? Then I take my thermometer out and proceed to take her temperature. This is where things went wrong. When I went to place the thermometer on her head, she jerked her head to the side, but didn't say a word. I assured her that it would not hurt and I was just taking her temperature, so I placed the thermometer back on her forehead and got a reading of 101.7. That in itself was not a big problem.

I then stated to her that she had a little fever. At that moment, in a scratchy, low voice, clear as a bell, she said, "The mention of the Lord makes me hot." Now, really, I'm not too sure what that was supposed to mean. All I know is I saw that same look in her eyes that I had seen the night before. I knew it was pure evil, and I freaked out! I know, '...greater is He that is in [me], than he that is in the world," (I John 4:4) but right now I'm thinking that I don't want any part of what is in this lady!

I darted toward the bathroom where my co-worker was getting the bath ready. She later told me she knew something was wrong by my facial expression. I just told her that I was out of there and if she didn't come with me, then she would be there alone. Well, it would have been unprofessional to leave my co-worker wondering where I disappeared to, right. She knew I was freaking out, so she tried to remain calm. She took the reins and talked some sense into me. She reminded me that since the patient was running fever, she did not have to take a bath. She said she could give her a quick sponge bath, and then we could leave. She point blank told me, "We came to do our job and we have to do it."

She was right, but I was all but kicking and screaming telling her to hurry up. She had me go find some clothes to put on the patient. She was finding anything to keep me busy. I just wanted out of there and was done with this patient. I have the best aide in the world! She was done with that bed bath in seven minutes!

As we were headed out, I took my thermometer and placed it on the patient's head. I just had to know if it would read different. It was reading 98.6. It took me five seconds to get to my car! From there, I called my registered nurse and expressed my concerns with the patient being left alone. She arrived thirty minutes later and discovered the gas to the kitchen stove was on and filling up the house. I can only speculate what that was all about, but I'm sure that spirit saw his time with her was ending soon. I feel it was an attempt on her life. Since she was in no condition to be home alone, she was taken to a nursing facility immediately.

That morning I had a long talk with God and my pastor. I was no good to anybody. I could not figure out why God would place me in that path. Why did I have to encounter this? I guess if I believe in good spirits at the end of life, I need to know there can be bad ones as well. So was this a mission? If so, I felt very ill-prepared. I received some very good scriptures and words of encouragement from my pastor. He can attest that I needed it!

The patient arrived at the nursing home where I felt a little better about seeing her. I gave myself a little time away from her. I needed to regroup and be strong again. When I finally went to make a visit, the patient never spoke a word to me. She did not make eye contact. I was a little puzzled by this. It was unsettling to assess someone that I knew was having issues with me. God just reminded me that she was His child and I needed to love her because He did.

The very next time I went to see her; I was at the nurse's station in the facility. I had other patients to see, but I knew my registered nurse was in the room talking with her. She'd told me for a week that there was nothing wrong with this lady. She said that the patient spoke with her all the time. Knowing this, I decide to be a little sneaky. I just had to know. This lady was messing with my head in a big way.

I walked quietly down the hall. I hid outside in the hallway. I was floored by what I heard. My co-worker, the registered nurse, was totally having a conversation with this patient. So after a few minutes, I thought I would come in on the conversation. I walked around the corner and entered the room. The patient looked my way, extended her neck tall, and turned her head away from me in a swift movement. She stayed that way until I left the room. She never said a word. I left that room knowing something wasn't right. I prayed a lot for God's guidance. I was a mess wondering why I was being put through this. I always covered myself and my family with Jesus' blood as I entered her room. She really made me aware of how important it is to keep your prayers from being hindered.

One day the sun shined all over this situation. I walked into her room as I had before, and she sat up on the side of her bed. I noticed that when I called her by her name, she would talk to me. She would interrupt herself during our conversations to turn her back toward me and say, in a rough voice, "You need to leave now." I would call her by her name again, and once again she would respond with kindness wanting to talk to me. I continued this because I felt as if I was pulling this lady out of something.

I finally got the courage to ask if I could pray with her. She responded by saying, "Please pray for me," but she immediately turned her back again and said in a louder voice, "It's time for you to go now," so I wasn't about to venture down this road alone. I called my wonderful pastor's wife to come help me pray. I felt inadequate at the time. This was big, in my book. I now know that I would've been just fine. It's not what we humans do that wakes up the spirit world, it is God working through us. When God is in control, things go very smoothly.

When my help arrived, we entered my patient's room and, in not so many words, my patient agreed to prayer. There were powerful prayers being poured out, and I know Jesus was so glad someone had reached this lady in time. My patient was so thankful for the prayers. Then she said something to me at that moment that confirmed in me what had happened. She looked at me and said, "I knew that first night I met you that you would help me." My heart instantly confirmed that I had been sent on a mission.

I always prayed with her after that, and she did go home to be with Jesus. I know where she is at and Who she is with. As much as I kicked, screamed and questioned God, I am so thankful that I had that experience. Spirits are real, whether they are good or bad. I now can say that I have personally experienced both. Not that I care to ever encounter bad spirits, but I feel I can better handle a tough situation if it means a soul will be saved.

True Love

This is a story about how God made things line up just right. We had a patient and he and his wife were as one. He had declined so much his wife was having a hard time caring for him. He was admitted to the nursing home for respite care. Respite care is just a short-term stay at a facility.

While he was in the facility, his doctor was there to make rounds. When the doctor came in to see the patient, the doctor quickly realized that the patient's wife was dehydrated and run down. The doctor admitted "her" to the hospital. After a lot of persuading, she agreed. She hated to leave her sick husband more than anything.

The next day I went to visit our patient in respite at the facility and observed that he did not have much time left. He had taken a quick turn and became an actively dying patient. We describe that a patient is actively dying when they display symptoms that indicate possibility of death in less than three days. All the children chose not to tell their mom, thinking they were protecting her. After convincing the children that their mother would want to know that her husband could pass at any time, I went to the hospital where the wife was admitted.

One of her daughters said the nurse would not call the doctor to get her mother released. The nurse stated that the doctor would be in later and she would ask him then. I knew that if the wife was not there with her husband when he passed, she would never forgive herself. She was not admitted for heart problems, just fatigue, so I saw no reason for her not to find out so she could hurry and get to her husband. I was on a mission now! This just wasn't right. Sometimes our job is to take care of more than just the physical needs of our patients.

After feeling a tug of urgency from the Holy Spirit, I took it upon myself to ask the nurse, "Are you calling the doctor or do I need to?" I meant business! She was very reluctant and aggravated, but she picked the phone up and called him. The doctor immediately agreed to release her from the hospital. Everyone knows a lot of paperwork comes next, but the nurse who had called the doctor for orders proceeded to lean back in her chair to do nothing. Let me remind you that a man is dying and his wife needs to get to him. This nurse was really not responding to the urgency of the situation.

When I asked what she was waiting on, she said her ward clerk, who was on break, would be there soon. Since I had worked at that hospital before, I knew this nurse was not in a hurry and I felt strongly that we needed to speed this along. I pleaded with the nurse to please get the paperwork done. I even volunteered to come behind the counter and help. She rolled her eyes and proceeded with the paperwork. She was not very happy with me, but my job was to take care of my patient's needs, not hers. The paperwork was finally done, and now the wife could get back to her husband! Not much time had really passed, but it seemed like an eternity trying to make sure the wife got back.

The most amazing part of this story is what happened when the patient's wife came back to the nursing home to be with her husband. She crawled up in bed with him, snuggling with her love of many years. He passed twenty minutes later! She was very thankful to have been with him.

Now this is why I love my job. I feel, with God's help, I made a difference in this situation. This is one of my favorite stories. They were very loving and caring to each other and everyone else. They deserved to spend those precious twenty minutes together.

Never-Ending

I feel I should try to come to an end, although there is no end in hospice. As long as there is life, there will be death. As long as there are deaths, there will be stories. I treasure each and every patient and their story. Only God can make these truly amazing events happen that I have written about. I pray that my eyes stay open and my heart stays in tune with the spirit that leads and guides me. Whether it's a positive experience or a more challenging experience, I know it's exactly what God wants me to have.

I started writing because I did not want to forget these awesome stories. Now, I feel that these stories may help someone else to draw close to the same God that I could not live without. The same God that speaks to my spirit can speak to yours. It only takes one small step of faith to start.

www.ingramcontent.com/pod-product-compliance
Lightning Source LLC
Chambersburg PA
CBHW060629030426
42337CB00018B/3266